Faith and Love

Moving Along Through Biblical Truth

Faith and Love

Moving Along Through Biblical Truth

Virginia Lee Edge

ARPress
45 Dan Road Suite 5
Canton MA 02021

Hotline: 1(888) 821-0229
Fax: 1(508) 545-7580

Ordering Information:
Quantity sales. Special discounts are available on quantity purchases by corporations, associations, and others. For details, contact the publisher at the address above.

Printed in the United States of America.
ISBN-13:   Paperback   979-8-89330-589-0
               eBook   979-8-89330-590-6

Library of Congress Control Number: 2024902581

Contents

Part 1

Faith and Love

INTRODUCTION

In the beginning He God created the heavens and the earth, and every splendid thing that could have inhabit this earth. But the most explicit gift to mankind is when our God created living beings, Adam and Eve. God formed these two living begins from the dirt of the ground and gave them his special breathe of Life as living souls.

It was a sin that changed the trajectory of man, which is a true statement. Meaning man's path and physical condition had changed, and God banished them from the Garden of Eden.

Figuratively speaking disobedience altered the course of our history, and doctrine. The serpent in the garden of Eden understood the function of mankind. What the serpent did was use the strategy of manipulation of man's seven (7) senses. These seven senses the serpent of the devil worked on, were the eyesight gate, hearing gate, taste gate, touch gate, smell gate, proprioception gate and the peripheral immune system gate. All seven of these senses work together. Like the proprioception gate allows for proper movement and positioning of your body and the peripheral immune system gate delivers all information to the brain and the body functions as one unit. The serpent knew that God had give Adam and Eve instruction not to eat or touch the tree of knowledge of good and evil. But the serpent manipulated their seven (7) senses. The true mistake Adam and Eve made was listing to the serpent going it alone, not calling on God for clarification and approval! This is how the serpent (devil) manipulated man, and still today.

History of Jesus, He was baptized to "fulfill all righteousness "(Matthew 3:15), He entered the priesthood forever after the order of Melchizedek (Psalm 110:4, Hebrew 5:8—10; 6:20). Jesus started His ministry around the age of thirty and was crucified around the age of thirty-three, and was offered as a sacrifice for our sins.

God's word says.

John 15:7

If ye abide in me, and my words abide in you, ye shall ask what ye will, and it shall be done unto you.

Ephesians 5:22

Wives, submit yourselves unto your own husbands, as unto the Lord.

First is your heart right with God. And do you have faith as a mustard seed, that you can tell a mountain in your life to move! That nothing will be impossible for you (Matthew 17:20). It is very important you read the Bible for understanding truly to know faith is.

Can you love your neighbor as God has taught all to do? Are you honoring God's words? If married, is your husband the head of your household as God is the head of the church? Can you be submissive to your husband? Do you think being submissive to your husband means you have lost control of your life?

A. What would your answers be, if you sat down to think about this?

Let your husband see Christ in you, humble yourself, that your pride will not give Satan access into your home (your life). Never point a finger at another human being, it will come back to punish you. Just continue to humble yourself, repent, and give all praise and honor to your father God (Jesus).

2. Chronicles 7:14

If my people, which are called by my name, shall humble themselves, and pray, and seek my face, and turn from their wicked ways; then will I hear from heaven, and will forgive their sin, and will heal their land.

The area in your life that you are being attacked is called a spiritual attack, it could present itself as a physical and even a mental attack. That's when you need to pick up your Bible and start feeding yourself with God's word, the devil (Satan) is afraid of the words of God. The devil knows he is no match for what God can dish out. But if you always try to go it alone in life, the devil will be at your door every time. Use scripture in your mouth to stop these spiritual attacks, God will always be with you to move those mountains in your life. Always call on Jesus who shed His blood for you…You are very special. Jesus is your Father, He shed His Blood for You!

Look where you are being attacked, like your marriage, finances or health, these are a few examples. Satan is a real enemy; he is always looking to deceive you. That's why you must call on Jesus any time of the day and follow Jesus. He shed His blood for us. He is our Father; Jesus has the final power don't entertain the devil's attacks – in Jesus Name.

Matthew 6:22

The light of the body is the eye if therefore thine eye be single, thy whole body shall be full of light.Luke 8:11

Now the parable is this: The seed is the word of God.

Luke 6:38

Give, and it shall be given unto you; good measure, pressed down, and shaken together, and running over, shall men give into your bosom, for with the same measure that ye mete withal it shall be measured to you again.

The only thing that travels around this world everyday freely is MONEY . . . it doesn't answer to no man, plus it doesn't have to pay for anything!

The greatest luxury in life that God (Jesus) has given us on this earth, is to have a great friend.

Chapter 1

The Gospel of Character

What makes a difference in a man's character, knowing the Holy Spirit and the word of God (Jesus). This is accomplished by listening and understanding the spoken word of God. The negative man focuses on the weakness of others and uses conversation to discredit another.

They use words of wisdom in a negative-positive way, and what the other person hears is the negative not the positive. They build you up, to tear you down with all the nice negativity that can be used. Never let any individual direct your life, you are the author of your life. God (Jesus) has made you perfect and wonderful in all his ways. The way you'll find the way to go, is through Gods (Jesus) word.

Psalm 51:10

Create in me a clean heart, O God; and renew a right spirit within me.

Psalm 51:11

Cast me not away from thy presence, and take not thy holy spirit from me.

John 10:30

I and my father are one.

Genesis 1:26

And God said, Let us make man in our image, after our likeness: and let them have dominion over the fish of the sea, and over the flow of the air, and over the cattle, and over all the earth, and over every creeping thing that creepeth upon the earth.

Genesis 1:27

So God created man in his own image, in the image God created he him; male and female created he them.

What travels around the world every day, and doesn't answer to any man?

Answer:_____

What is the greatest luxury in life that God has given us on this earth?
Answer:_____

Chapter 2

Success

Seize the opportunity, Yes success is a mindset. Belief is the seed for prosperity, no one achieves prosperity or success without being of service to another. People don't believe what you say until they know what you can do, and if you care, and have integrity.

All successful people became successful because they gave of their talents and ability in the service of others. You can contribute in some way to others no matter how great or small your talents, you too can become successful.

How to develop a successful individual, by encouragement and great time spent to integrate massive amount of information, in reading, language skills, that the individual is curious able. This prepares the brain for deep learning of un-memorized information they will retain. The ways of success is related to your ability to integrate new knowledge and learning to understand with an open mind, to the information you receive without prejudice, to impart wisdom and understanding.

Remember, the world hates change, yet it is the only thing that has brought progress, the change. Remember, there is nothing permanent except change because it will always happen. Times change and we change with it, sometimes it's for the better other times, we just can't tell.

Change takes place around our reality and our commitments. You can start with one person to institute change, and end up with a life of success, or do nothing, and never move anywhere. Any man's life can be changed for the better, the answers are all in God's word, read for yourself to edify your body and mind.

Proverbs 22:7

The rich ruleth over the poor, and the borrower is servant to the lender.

Proverbs 22: 8

He that soweth iniquity shall reap vanity: and the rod of his anger shall fail.

Proverbs 22:9

He that hath a bountiful eye shall be blessed; for he giveth of his bread to the poor.

Proverbs 22:1

A good name is rather to be chosen than great riches, and loving favor rather than silver and gold.

Proverbs 22:2

The rich and poor meet together: the Lord is the maker of them all.

Chapter 3

Practical Knowledge

Practical knowledge never stops learning and acquiring specialized knowledge.

a. The major purpose of schooling gives practicalknowledge.

b. To become successful at anything, you must be self-discipline to stay focus.

c. A precious stone cannot be polished without friction nor humanity perfected without trials.

The philosophy and purpose of the group are to strengthen the character, by doing so you specialize in a different knowledge base and understanding of each individual.

If you speak to people that are not happy, and you truly listen. You will hear what is not being said or expressed. Remember, God (Jesus) is always to be your source, always find out what the word of God (Jesus) has to say.

John15:7

If you abide in me, and my words abide in you, ye shall ask what ye will, and it shall be done unto you.

Remember knowledge and wisdom cometh by hearing and reading the word of God.

God (Jesus) speaks to you through His words. Sit down with God (Jesus) and His words will be food for your soul . . . He talks to you.

God talks to us always through scriptures, through other people that cross our lives in daily encounters. Through our dreams, and an audible voice that is felt within our spirit!

Quotes:

Billy Grham: "The gift of knowledge is the supernatural ability to impart a special word of wisdom into a situation. It's also the ability to speak wisely and knowingly about a situation with truth from the Bible."

Billy Graham: "describes the gift of knowledge in his book "The Holy Spirit" as, "That knowledge which is the gift of the Spirit is based on long hours of disciplined study in which God teaches us."

1 Corinthians 12:1 Now concerning spiritual gifts, brethren, I would not have you ignorant.

1 Corinthians 12:2 Ye Know that ye were Gentiles, carried away unto these dumb idols, even as ye were led.

1 Corinthians 12: 3 Wherefore I give you to understand that no man speaking by the spirit of God calleth Jesus accursed: and that no man can say that Jesus is the Lord, but by the Holy Ghost.

God has given each of us the gift of the Holy Spirit, there are seven gifts: wisdom, understanding, counsel, fortitude, knowledge, piety, and fear of the Lord.

And we are many members in one body, so is Christ many members.

1 Corinthians 12:27 Now ye are the body of Christ, and members in particular.

Ephesians 5:30 For we are members of this body, of his flesh, and of his bones.

Ephesians 5:31 FOR THIS CAUSE SHALL MAN LEAVE HIS FATHER AND MOTHER, AND SHALL BE JOINED UNTO HIS WIFE, AND THEY SHALL BE ONE FLESH.

Chapter 4

Imagination

In your own right, there is no limitation. When one accumulates one's wealth your, self-worth improves, and your net-worth and overall financial health get better. Remember, you control your future and destiny when you're following God's (Jesus) word. What you think about comes about.

When your imagination runs wild and branches off into different levels of possibilities, self-worth improves, and you can prosper beyond belief. Because you now believe in yourself to step out and take the chance on your own.

Remember, you control your future and destiny when you're following God's (Jesus) word. What you think about comes about.

By recording your dreams and goals on paper, you are setting in motion the process of becoming the person you most want to be. Put your future in God's hands . . . you own your life, it's a gift from God (Jesus).

Do not let money be your focus if you do not have any, God will show you the way once you are willing to step out of your comfort zone. God will put someone or thing in your life to make it happen for you!

An old saying I use to hear is this:

"If you think you are beaten, you are. If you think you are not, your not. If you like to win, but you think you can't, it is almost certain you won't. If you think you'll lose, you're lost.

For out of the world we find, success begins with a fellow's will. It's all in the state of mind. If you think you are out of class, you are, you've got to think high to rise, you've got to be sure of yourself before, you can ever win a prize. Life's battles don't always go to the stronger or faster man. But soon or later the man who wins is the man who Thinks He Can!"

Another old saying that I heard:

Thoughts become Words

Words become Actions

Actions become Habits

Habits become Character

The character becomes your Destiny

So go win the war in your mind and start thinking that you can!

Proverbs 23:7 As he thinketh in his heart, so is he: Eat and drink, saith he to thee, but his heart is not with thee.

Proverbs 23:8 The morsel which thou has eaten shall thou vomit up, and lose thy sweet words.

Proverbs 23:9 Speak not in the ears of a fool: for he will despise the wisdom of thy words.

The tone of this I say in your imagination is: Keep your business to yourself and wait till your seed is planed firmly in the ground and is ready to sprout wings. Before you tell all your business.

Bible Says:

Proverbs 13:3 He that keepeth his mouth keepeth his life: but he that openeth wide his lips shall have destruction.

Ephesians 4:29 Let no corrupt communication proceed out of your mouth, but that which is good to the use of edifying, that it may minister grace unto the hearers.

Chapter 5

Thoughts

Thoughts are what you want, your desires determine your thoughts, persistence is your burning desire to win, and faith is definitely what you need, and love is a prerequisite. So, hand your prescription in now to God (Jesus), and let Him fill your prescription, it will cost you nothing . . . but faith and love.

Remember life is in God(Jesus), God (Jesus) is love, plant your seeds first, before you start your journey. God(Jesus) said I'm finished, there is no life in this world without Him.

So, never stop dreaming, never stop believing in yourself . . . you can do great things in life . . . give all to God (Jesus) in faith and love . . . because He can handle all!

John 10:30

I and my father are one.

Learn how to serve God first, once on God's side, you will find life more abundant.

While it's still day you must work, while you are alive, you must do the work of God (Jesus). Every one of us has been called by God (Jesus) to do His work. We are servants as a people, and we must give service to God (Jesus) all the days of our lives.

Remember, our battle is not with the Lord, It's with the principalities (Satan) of this earth.

Remember, before King David was a King, he used a slingshot and a stone to slay the giant. When the stone left his sling, it left David's control into God's control.

We all have giants in our lives today, let loose. and give God (Jesus) control.

Let's expound on this a little, the giant above can be any problem in your life. When you release your stone (the problem), you are releasing the problem into God's hands, into His control. Most people try handling problems on their own . . . this is not good.

You need to release whatever it is into God's (Jesus) hands, He is the author and the finisher of it all.

You need help, then trust (have faith) God (Jesus) at his word. Let's start together, God (Jesus) is at the head. When you release your life to God (Jesus), He releases blessing and favor into your (by your faith) life.

Remember, God (Jesus) always requires our involvement, we release our faith and God (Jesus) will take it from there. You will see, how God (Jesus) will direct your life, it will always be for the better. Remember God's (Jesus) ways are not our ways, and God's thoughts are not like our thoughts.

Let's use the example of your tithe, this is your stone(your seed). You need to release it to God (Jesus), and God (Jesus) releases your blessing one by one. There is a blessing in the stone (your seed,) that you need to sow. The principle here is to sow your seed (the stone) and break the curse off your life.

Don't carry a curse on your life, for the lack of knowledge of God's (Jesus) true word of the tithe. You work for money, now let money work for you. When you do not trust in God, you miss what God's (Jesus) life plans are for you financially and health- wise. Stop trying to handle everything yourself, give it all to the Master-God (Jesus) and let Him show you a better way.

Chapter 6

Love

What is it? Love is God (Jesus), God (Jesus) is love, there is no other definition for God's (Jesus) love. God's (Jesus) love is unconditional, the church is founded and grounded on the love of God (Jesus).

Unconditional love keeps marriages together and strong. Love does not boast in itself. This love must be passed to all generations. They must know the fruits of this love and where it comes from. They must know the first fruit of the spirit is love. You don't have to puff up love, it's love unconditional, no strings attached . . . love does not behave itself unseen.

Love never disappears when you need it, love stays together in all things. Love meets challenges head-on, love does not insult, love does not cut you down in public, love is unconditional.

Remember, your words are spirit, you can have what you say. When you have unconditional love and walking upright with God (Jesus).

Matthew 16:19

And I will give unto thee the keys of the kingdom of heaven: and what so ever thou shalt bind on earth shall be bound in heaven: and what so ever thou shalt loose on earth shall be loosed in heaven.

Luke 10:19

Behold, I give unto you power to tread on serpents and scorpions, and over all the power of the enemy: and nothing shall by any means hurt you.

Let your light so shine in unconditional love – spread God's word. He is our seasoning -and God will never lose His flavor – because no man can chance Him – What a Powerful statement – NO MAN CAN CHANCE OUR GOD!

Let us get our seasoning from the Bible – because salt never loses its strength when it is God's word – God is our judge reading the Bible we learn to bridle our tongues – AMEN!

Let us continue to season our words with love we are each responsible for knowing what God's word means. Some people may quote God's word for word but not understand. We are all responsible to ask God about his word if we do not clearly understand for edification.

There is man's wisdom in this world, but we need to ask God for his wisdom on how to truly love one another and walk in this true love.

Chapter7

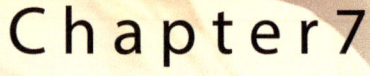

Self-Assurance and Self-Confidence

The worse day in your life is the best in your life. Point to your life and say, I am going to be famous one day . . . I'm going to be very rich one day. Call on your faith in God (Jesus), speak to your Holy Spirit in you.

Remember, being rich and famous doesn't always have to mean money, it could mean health, it could mean you became famous because you invented something that helps mankind.

All honor and glory should be given unto God for all that He does for you from day today. Because God supplies all the oxygen that we live by from day to day. Just make a list of all God (Jesus) continues to do!

You are sure of yourself and you are confident that God is with you every step of the way!

You know why because God loves His children. And every child of God's should feel his love! God gave his only son Jesus Christ to die for our sins on the cross and He still loves us all. Even as we still sin today.

Chapter 8

✦ ✚ ✦

Your Storms in Life

What are your storms in life, don't worry be happy, and just let it go. Sit down and have your conference with God (Jesus) and continue in the essence of your day, without looking back. Start helping yourself by planting your seeds and sowing every day into other lives, be a blessing into someone else's life.

The enhancement comes with your original mission and the correct attitude. The correct attitude corrects your emotions, by your relationship with God (Jesus). All we need is faith, as small as a mustard seed, to bring about change in our lives.

When thinking, of a grain of a mustard seed, and you try to equate this with the world's religion. You have to wonder, what is so wrong with this world system and why, is there so much distention among the world religion.

A. The answer is, a lot of us do not have faith for the mustard seed. . . to move those mountains.

Where can we get this faith from, and how can we keep this faith?

A. The answers are in God's (Jesus) word, as you read, He will teach you.

There are so many different religions in this world. It's imaginable that we as God's (Jesus) children, can't get along.

In this world, there is only one higher power, and it's God (Jesus). A power that is greater than any man can stand up against, he is God (Jesus)and the <u>WORD</u> was with God.

So storms that come and go in our lives, we must let go and let God truly handle it. Prayer is a powerful weapon – AMEN!

Chapter 9

---✛✛✛---

Bear Witness

Our God (Jesus) bears witness to all creation, and what a creation. Can anyone man duplicate this world?

A. The answer is, NO.

Man cannot even recognize, emotionally or psychologically the vase power beyond this earth (the world) or even inside this earth. God (Jesus) has allowed man to have earthly skills and knowledge, which are not of His Kingdom.

We, as God's (Jesus) children, must not lean on our understanding. You can be sure that God (Jesus) knows and hears all of our daily concerns. If you need to hear from God (Jesus), you must read His Word, and leave all your concerns in his hands.

A. If, you want to hear from God (Jesus) pick up the Bible and read His word.

God's (Jesus) word does not teach hate, it does not teach you religion. God's word, teaches you to love one another and so much more.

Look at all of us, we are all God's (Jesus) children, we are like a rainbow of different colors, all different nationalities, shapes, heights, and sizes. We speak hundreds of different languages, we have different forms of religious practices, and we still war against each other.

We have been privileged to be witness to all that God (Jesus) has created, to be His children that have been given dominion over all, as it says in Genesis 1:26.

Genesis 1:26

And God said, Let us make man in our image, after our likeness: and let them have dominion over the fish of the sea, and over the fowl of the air, and over the cattle, and over all the earth, and over every creeping thing that creepeth upon the earth.

The bible says in Genesis 1:26, Let us make man in our image, after our likeness.

Then why in God's (Jesus) name is there so much hate and evil in this society?

A. Answer: All man don't know of God's (Jesus) <u>WORD</u>, hate and blood does not dwell in God's (Jesus) word, He wants us to love one another.

Let God's (Jesus) word bear witness on this, whenever God (Jesus) saw evil he spoke on it.

John 3:17

For God sent not his Son into the world to condemn the world, but that the world through him might be saved.

God(Jesus), didn't look at the government as evil, he looked at the individual. The individual is evil because the word is not planted in him.

Why, is the government slowly (meticulously) moving God's (Jesus) word out of everything?

A. The answer is simple, it's because their deeds are corrupt and evil, they are continuously seeking more power and more money, they respect the positions of others less and less.

It makes it easy to do wrong without daily reminders of God's (Jesus) word in the courts, in the schools, etc.

Just look at our government, the Republicans and the Democrats can't even see eye to eye. Neither side has respect for their heads of state, does this sound familiar, they crucified Christ Jesus, verbally and physically. "PLEASE PRAY"

Proverbs 22:6

Train up a child in the way he should go: and when he is old, he will not depart from it.

All mankind regardless of their stations (positions) in life, need to work together for the betterment of this country. There is so much strife, resentment, and hate in the world's society with very little harmony working together.

Our children are our future, negativity discourages and causes disassociation with relationships with other people, and will hurt future generations to come. Just look at how our family units are today.

Children (young adults) mostly take on the characteristics of their parents, that's the world they see growing up, in the household.

If negativity and hate are being taught, this is the one example of what they perceive and learn.

The worldwide media is now part of all our families, it's turned on daily in our homes, the news is broadcast in detail. Our children are sponges, taking it all in, looking at the examples of their society and parents, what they say, what their lifestyles are, and how they cope with different issues.

These children are even paying more attention today, to the government's political arena. To the children, this must look like a war in progress. Our government political arena doesn't even show respect for any one person's position.

To move in the direction that God has intended for us . . . we have to keep moving towards what we know is right in the love of course. We have to have faith that God has all of the answers for every situation, detail, and aspect of our lives.

Truth especially biblical is not always an easy pill to swallow . .

. but it is always good for us and good to us. Gods' word is the same yesterday, today and forever and it is no respecter of men, so it is what it is and what it is – is necessary!

Since our children are the greatest gift that God has entrusted to us, we need to be sure to handle them in the manner that will please God (who is the truth and the light).

One of the biggest truths that we need to move into is the eliminating the NO factor . . . allowing children to say "No" when you give them direction, ask them to do something or just plain rearing .

. . is not acceptable and it is not cute. A child needs to be loving and obedient; they need to learn to listen the first time.

Countdowns are the beginning of a breakdown. When a child knows they will get you to say – ONE . . . TWO . . . and you better be moving when I get to T . . . H . . . R . . . E . . . E – you are teaching your child that they have time to think about disobeying what you have told them to do.

Let your yes be yes and your No is No. God gives us specific instructions to "Train up a child in the way he should go: and when he is old, he will not depart from it."

Proverbs 22:6. Well, that training includes not allowing your child to run and rule you or your household.

Children need to be respectful and obedient and proper discipline in love will ensure that you are in God's will.

We must teach our children to have integrity in all that they do. That integrity comes from watching parents that are great role models and from constant immersion and practical application of Gods' word daily.

They must respect you as the authoritative figure in their lives. If your child doesn't learn proper respect, they will grow to disregard authority.

Authority is everywhere we go, and whether we admit it or not, we are subjected to it. And whether we admit it or not, we are subject to it. I have always said that RESPECT is not an option. To get the respect you must give it and when we submit to authority in the proper way . . . we always do it with integrity and respect.

When you have multiple children you have to be sure to treat each child individually and with equitable amounts of love. This will help to avoid unhealthy jealousy among the children.

Jealousy is an awful thing in anger and you never want it to rear its green head. Our children need to learn to share and sharing goes far beyond " you hold it for 3 minutes and I hold it for 3 minutes", they also need to know that "I, the Lord your God, am a jealous God." Exodus 20:5.

Our kids need to know that God wants all of them . . . just like he wants all of us. God wants us to seek him and find him, put Him first in all that we do, honor our mother and father and God's jealousy is the only healthy kind. Integrity and loyalty as biblical truths are both best seen than talked about.

When a child sees great adult examples of Integrity and loyalty, which is worth 1000 words. Children are like sponges, they absorb everything from the environment around them. Little things like promising to take your daughter for ice cream if she gets a great report card or helping a friend move at the date, time, and place that you say you will are great examples of your integrity and loyalty to them and others.

Children don't like broken promises—neither do we to say the least.

In Titus 2:7 it says "in all things showing yourself to be a pattern of good works; in doctrine showing integrity, reverence, incorruptibility" . . . wow we want to show a great pattern – which means to do it over and over again.

Without fail we should be men and women of our word, especially when we say or promise something to our children. Our casual treatment of our words and actions to our children will cause them to be slack and disregard the value of their words and promises.

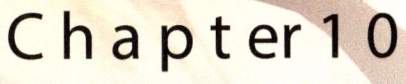

Chapter 10

Man's Words Proceeds its Self

A man's words can proceed itself, but if the heart of man is not pure (sincere) he can spoil the fruit of his own house.

If your heart is not pure (sincere) on the points you make to your families, and to your fellow man, dissension creeps in, and the holy spirit bears witness to all man.

Let's all pray that the Republicans, Democrats, and the President of the United States of America, can resolve their issues and see eye to eye, for all mankind, let God's (Jesus) word edify their minds and body.

God's (Jesus) word teaches man through faith and love. God's love is not your dictionary kind of love, it's God's unconditional love that man has to learn throughout the study of the Bible (God's Word).

Choose to have a personal conversation with God. Learn to listen closely to His word, ask for wisdom and understanding of His word.

God will never tell you to disrespect another man in any situation, that's the trick of Satan.

Satan is the author of confusion, we must always be ready as it says in the Bible:

Ephesians 6:12—18

For we wrestle not against flesh and blood, but against principalities, against powers, against the rulers of the darkness of the world, against spiritual wickedness in high places. Wherefore take unto you the whole armour of God, that ye may be able to withstand in the evil day, and having done all, to stand.

Stand therefore, having your loins girt about with truth, and having on the breastplate of righteousness;

And your feet shod with the preparation of the gospel of peace;

Above all, taking the shield of faith, wherewith ye shall be able to quench all the fiery darts of the wicked.

And take the helmet of salvation, and the sword of the spirit, which is the word of God:

Praying always with all prayer and supplication in the spirit, and watching thereunto with all perseverance and supplication for all saints.

Remember Christ Jesus said:

John 14: 15

If you love me, keep my commandments.

John 15:10

If ye keep my commandments, ye shall abide in my love; even as I have kept my Father's commandments, and abide in his love.

Chapter 11

❖✚✚✚❖

Your Desire

Your desire should be to learn more of God's (Jesus) word than ever before. God's (Jesus) word speaks understanding to your spirit.

A burning desire gives you the energy and will power, the effort to dream great dreams and find a new purpose in your life.

You have a right to your own opinion, but not to your truth, because God (Jesus) is the only one that knows the truth.

Always season your speech (words), with love. Be harder on yourself than you are on others.

I Corinthians 13:6

Rejoiceth not in iniquity, but rejoiceth in the truth.

I Corinthians 13:7

Beareth all things, believeth all things, hopeth all things, endureth all things.

I Corinthians 14:1

Follow after charity, and desire spiritual gifts, but rather that ye may prophesy.

I Peter 2:2

As a newborn babes, desire the sincere milk of the word, that ye may grow thereby.

Your eyes are the light to the soul. Judge not, and you shall not be judged. When you get busy for God (Jesus) he makes provisions for you.

God (Jesus) gives us power over all our enemies. In the name of Jesus, the devil is subject unto Jesus.

In everything you do or schedule to do, for example like a vacation, you should always say, If the Lord wills . . . we will be going to Hawaii on vacation in Jesus name.

Chapter 12

❖━✦━✛⊕✛━✦━❖

How do we save life's

We save lives by being a blessing to others, by being doers of the word. If you can help someone, then that person soon learns through God's love of the word to help someone else with the same unconditional love.

We save lives by being a blessing and by walking by faith and love. Never overlooking anything you know is not right, because it will multiple if not corrected.

Self-worth comes from my God, and you're the one that matters most to God (Jesus).

Your value is never lost because you are God's masterpiece. Everything has value, the Olive tree was used in the manager for Christ Jesus's birth.

The Oaktree was used when Jesus needed a boat on the water. The pine tree was used as a cross when Jesus was crucified.

God is not in control of everything, the example he gives you free will to choose.

Wisdom teaches, it's the study of differences in man's judgment, these differences decide your status in life, through your growth in the word of God (Jesus).

God will teach you anything you would like to know, just sow your way out of trouble, and pray without ceasing.

God (Jesus) says heaven and earth shall pass away, but my words shall not pass away.

Psalm 23:1—6

The Lord is my shepherd; I shall not want.

He marketh me to lie down in green pastures: he leadeth me beside the still waters.

He restoreth my soul: he leadeth me in the paths of righteousness for his name's sake.

Yea, though I walk through the valley of the shadow of death, I will fear no evil: for thou art with me; thy rod and thy staff they comfort me.

Thou prepares a table before me in the presence of mine enemies: thou anointest my head with oil; my cup runneth over.

Surely goodness and mercy shall follow me all the days of my life: and I will dwell in the house of the Lord for ever.

Chapter 13

The Essence of Man

The essence of man is his Faith and Love for God. What is the truth, it's simple, truth is what each man makes it, but it's not God's truth.

What is love, it's simple, love is what each man makes it, but it's not God's love.

What is life, it's simple, life is what each man makes it out to be, but it's not God's life for us.

Love is what you give into life unconditionally. Faith and love are what you find when you are reading God's (Jesus) word.

How do we find what we need in life? Well, that's simple, we find what we need through God's (Jesus) word. When Jesus was crucified, He left the Holy Spirit as a comforter for all mankind, to teach and guide us.

Do you believe the Holy Spirit is in you . . . most people don't believe. That's because, people can not justify what they can't see, feel or audibly hear. A lack of knowledge of God's (Jesus) word keeps them blind and as lost souls.

Remember, God (Jesus) is real, as Satan is real as Germs are real. The effects of all three are different, but, you can't see either one. Germs can destroy the body over time if a man doesn't take care of his health. Satan, slowly destroys man, out of greed, and man's lack of knowledge of God's (Jesus) word. God (Jesus), through His word, teaches us faith and love.

Many times, what a man thinks of himself, is based on the value on the outside and not the value that is within. Man, for example, is not poor until he thinks himself poor, it's all in his state of mind.

It's not the appearance of a man that's important, it's the state of the man that's more important. Man, needs God's (Jesus) word in his life, more than he can ever imagine.

No man should not be considered stupid in this world, in our eyes, God (Jesus) gives all men special gifts, some have more gifts (talent) than others. The gift that man has is to be used to service all mankind.

One should never think himself better (higher)than another, this leaves room for Satan to come in and destroy thy house. When thoughts of such, come into your mind, bind Satan from your mind, lose from Heaven positive words and blessings into your life and family.

Because Satan comes to destroy your seed (family) through the words of your mouth. Satan, plants ideas and you act upon them, you have allowed Satan to plant these seeds of destruction in your mind. Don't berate yourself, you need to know the truth, and it's to lose God's (Jesus) words in your heart and mind.

Isaiah 55:8

For my thoughts are not your thoughts neither are your ways my ways, saith the Lord.

We, all need to grow more in God's (Jesus) obedience . . . through His authority and power of His word.

God will always put one or more people in your life for a season to bless your life. You need to keep planting your seeds for that harvest and expect a great harvest of miracles in your life and for your family's life.

Matthew 18:18

Verily I say unto you, whatsoever ye shall bind on earth shall be bound in heaven: and whatsoever ye shall loose on earth shall be loosed in heaven.

Matthew 18:19

Again I say unto you, That if two of you shall agree on earth as touching any thing that they shall ask, it shall be done for them of my Father which is in heaven.

Matthew 18:20

For where two or three are gathered together in my name, there am I in the midst of them.

Chapter 14

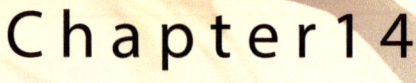

Un-Godly Ways

You can not justify what is not of God. Jesus is in his father's house and he is equal with his father. Un-Godliness would not be approved by God (Jesus).

We support the kingdom of God (Jesus) on this earth by those who are believers in God (Jesus).

God gives us a lot more than money, he gives us life, the holy spirit, health, wisdom, understanding . . . and many more gifts and blessings.

We are the temple of the Holy Spirit, we are the walking breathing church. God (Jesus) when crucified left the comforter with us.

John 6:35

Jesus said, I am the bread of life: he that cometh to me shall never hunger, and he that believeth on me shall never thirst.

John 10:11

Jesus said, I am the good shepherd: the good shepherd giveth his life for the sheep.

John 14:6

Jesus said, I am the way, the truth and the life: no man cometh unto the Father, but by me

Chapter 15

A Story

There was once a man of meager means, who wanted to join a church of great wealth. When he went to the church to join as a member, he was asked to fill out a church application for membership.

After the church board had reviewed his information, he was denied membership to this church. The man then left the church very upset and was crying while outside standing in front of the church.

A man comes up behind him and taps him on his shoulder. Sir, is there a problem, can I help. The man reply's, I wanted to join this church, but they wouldn't accept me. The man who tapped him on his shoulder was Jesus Christ. He said, don't feel bad they wouldn't let me in either.

John 5:41

I receive not honor from men.

John 5:42

But I know you, that ye have not love of God in you.

John 5:43

I am come in my Father's name, and ye receive me not: if another shall come in his own name, him ye will receive.

Roman 13:10

Love worketh no ill to his neighbour: therefore love is the fulfilling of the law.

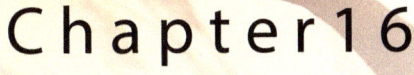

Chapter16

---◆—┼✠┼—◆---

In the Beginning, God sets up Laws

The Law of God to Adam:

Genesis 2:16

And the Lord God commanded the man, saying, Of every tree of the garden thou mayest freely eat:

Genesis 2:17

But of the tree of the knowledge of good and evil, thou shalt not eat of it, for in the day that thou eatest thereof thou shalt surely die.

The Law of God to Noah:

Genesis 9:6

Whoso sheddeth man's blood, by man shall his blood be shed: for in the image of God made he man.

The Law of God to Moses, laws of Moses to the Israelites:

Ex 20:2—17, Psalm 78:5, Matthew 5:18, Psalm 19:8, Romans

7:14, Romans 7:12,

1Timothy 1:8, Psalm 119:96, Psalm 19:7, Romans 12:2, Psalm

119:142,

Galatians 3:24, Deuteronomy 27:26, Psalm 51:6, Ecclesiastes

12:13, Matthew 5:28,

Matthew 22:37, Galatians 3:10, James 2:10, Romans 13:8,

Romans 13:10,

1Kings 8:46, Ecclesiastes 7:20, Romans 3:9—10, Romans 3:19,

Romans 7:5, Romans 8:7, Romans 2:12, James 2:10,

1 John 3:4, Acts 13:39, Romans 3:20,

Romans 3:38, Galatians2:16, Galatians 3:11, Romans 2:15,

Roman 3:20,

Romans 4:15, Romans 5:12—14.

Note there is approximately 270 law of Moses from God, I have noted 57 of them here for you to read, I know you will find the rest . . . God's (Jesus) blessings to you.

Chapter 17

Is a Governing Body necessary to run Society

If this was a perfect society, we would not need a governing body of rules and law. But, since it's not a perfect society, yes, we need a governing body to enforce these rules and laws.

Society, could not function if individuals had the freedom to do whatever they pleased. For example, the constitution and the federal law are the supreme laws of the land, no law may contradict the constitution.

These laws add consequences for anyone trying to breaking them., and a lot of these laws leave much room for interpretation.

You also need a governing force to set up jails and prisons to establish a society of control and order.

Prison's today are money-making Institutional businesses, you can find prisons owned under corporate names on the stock exchange.

Chapter 18

Reliable Parents

Back then ninety percent of the parents were reliable responsible adults. But, now when you look around, you have lost who is the adult and who is the child.

When you look around, young boys and young girls are having babies and they are not ready for parenting and playing house. Most of them have not finished school or have jobs. They have to rely on family support and welfare assistance.

They are not full-time parenting because the responsibilities now are too much for them. They still want to go out with their friends instead of their parents letting them know your baby is your responsibility. And the only time their parent is to take care of the Grandchild is if their daughter is going back to school to complete her education and or go to college and the young father is staying in school to complete his education and or go to college too!. That is when a parent should help and not make them lazy.

Parents need to look for a positive outcome. To, encourage these kids that they can have a great life by following their dreams and discipline themselves. In the long run, they will have a better outcome, that one day they can properly financially care for their child and themselves! This is a view from the other side of the bridge (that young people can not see – get them there)!

They should not be forced to get married, they may have never been in love and you would not want the relationship to turn into an abusive one and the child would suffer.

Children today, do not know much about their bodies and the Word of God's Bible that can teach them in the way they should go, to educate themselves. The word of God gives you the wisdom, understanding, and insight you need, to not be afraid to ask questions and step out of your comfort zone.

Because the world is not over for them (let them know that)!

And to let them know what unconditional love and true love are about, that one day they will be able to train up their children in the way they should go with God (Jesus) as their Pilot.

The point is how do we rebuild a stronger society on this earth? First, we need rules and a stronger governing body in place to meet the needs of our struggling economy and our deteriorating infrastructure.

Secondly, the government needs to position itself as one governing body (just listen to the news) to get things done.

When Jesus came to earth he brought a governing body. Jesus said my Kingdom is not of this world…but when the man lost the word of God (Jesus) they lost the truth!

The Church today cannot govern itself by earthy rules, because God's (Jesus) kingdom is not of this world, and we are governed by the word of God (Jesus).!

The Church is God's People! And the physical building where they assemble is to administer God's word…AMEN!

Praying that our young people get wiser and smarter, and get to know God's Word for themselves.

Read for understanding, and make your lives a beautiful picture that you will love and truly understand. Because the ability is there, just cross that bridge! **Of unconditional Power**!

God Bless Much Love from the Author of this book:

Faith and Love…Moving Along Through Biblical Truth.

Question and Answers

The point is, How do we rebuild a strong society on this earth.? First, we know rules and government need to be in place. The government needs to respect the position and the offices of the governing body (just listen to the news).

Answer:……………………………………………………

When Jesus came to earth he brought a governing body? Jesus said my kingdom is not of this earth but when a man lost the word of God (Jesus) they lost the truth.

Answer:……………………………………………………

The church today can not govern itself by earthy rules, because God's (Jesus) kingdom is not of this world, and we are governed by the word of God (Jesus).

Answer:……………………………………………………

YOUR ANSWERS MAY BE DIFFERENT

Chapter 19

Famous Quotes

Martin Luther King, Jr.:

"Hatred paralyzes life; love releases it. Hatred confuses life, love harmonizes it. " "Hatred darkens life; love illuminates it."

Martin Luther King:

"Everybody can be great . . . because anybody can serve. You don't have to have a college degree to serve. You don't have to have your subject and verb agree to serve. You only need a heart full of grace, a soul generated by love."

Nelson Mandela:

"Our deepest fear is not that we are inadequate. Our deepest fear is that we are powerful beyond measure. It is our light, not our darkness, that most frightens us. Your playing small does not serve the world. There is nothing enlightened about shrinking so that other people won't feel insecure around you. We are all meant to shine as children do."

"It's not just in some of us; it is in everyone. And as we let our own lights shine, we unconsciously give other people permission to do the same. As we are liberated from our own fear, our presence automatically liberates others."

Nelson Mandela:

"If you talk to a man in a language he understands, that goes to his head. If you talk to him in his language that goes to his head."

Nelson Mandela:

"Education is the most powerful weapon which you can use to change the world."

Oprah Winfrey:

Think like a queen. A queen is not afraid to fail, failure is another stepping stone to greatness."

Oprah Winfrey:

"I was raised to believe that excellence is the best deterrent to racism and sexism."

Oprah Winfrey:

"Turn your wounds into wisdom"

Oprah Winfrey:

"If you want to accomplish the goals of your life, you have to begin with the spirit."

Warren Buffett:

"Price is what you pay. Value is what you get"

Education:

"Ignorance never settles a question, life is my college. May I graduate well, and earn some honors."

Education:

"Children are educated by what the grown-up is and not by his talk."

Education:

"A child misadjusted is a child lost."

Education:

"All of life is a constant education."

Faith:

"What is essential is invisible to the eye."

Faith:

"Belief is when someone else does the thinking, faith is much better than belief."

Ability:

"To know how to hide one's ability is a great skill."

Dreams:

To accomplish great things we must not only act but also dream, not only plan but also believe."

Dreams:

In dreams and in love there are no impossibilities."

Jewish Proverb Quote:

"If your heart is bitter, sugar in your mouth will no help"

Jewish Proverb Quote:

"Man drives, but the creator holds the reins."

Jewish Proverb Quote:

"One should not stand at the foot of a sick person's bed, because that place is reserved for the guardian angel."

Jewish Proverb Quote:

"No one can make you feel inferior without your consent."

Jewish Proverb Quote:

"Pray not for things, but for wisdom and courage."

Jewish Proverb Quote:

"A half-truth is a whole lie."

Jewish Proverb Quote:

"I felt sorry for myself because I had no shoes-until I met a man who had no feet."

Jewish Proverb Quote:

"Man thinks, God laughs."

Jewish Proverb Quote:

"In choosing a friend, go up a step."

Jewish Proverb Quote:

"If God lived on earth people would break his windows." My Quotes

Virginia Edge:

Freely gift another through your giving.

Virginia Edge:

A relationship with unconditional love can endure all things.

Virginia Edge:

You need to be responsible for yourself.

Virginia Edge:

Keep your business to yourself.

Virginia Edge:

Mind your business.

Virginia Edge:

My color doesn't define me, my response does.

Virginia Edge:

Life is a recipe that can be found in any Bible because God (Jesus) never changes.

Virginia Edge:

Hunger Hates Waste.

Virginia Edge:

Be a Blessing to Someone Else.

Virginia Edge:

Love is not blind, but you sure need Sunshades.

Part 2

For anyone Who has Read this Book

God Bless And Much Love!

Virginia L. Edge has been a sponsor for children at World Vision, building a better world for children, for the past twenty-two years, since 06/04/1999. If you are interested in sponsoring a child from any part of the world, you can write or call world vision, or go to their website, as follows:

World Vision
P.O.Box 70029
Tacoma, WA 98481-0029
Ph: 1-888-511-6534
Website: WWW.WorldVision.Org

Virginia L. Edge, donates to the Mercy Ship program that follows the 2000 - year – old model of Jesus to provide hope and healing to the world's forgotten poor.

For over 40 years, Mercy Ship has offered medical services across the globe, giving confidence to millions who struggle to survive and have limited or no access to healthcare. Mercy Ships serves all people without regard for race, gender, or religion.

(MercyShip.org)

MercyShip P.O.Box 1930
Garden Valley, TX 75771-1930

Part 3

About the Author

Virginia Edge the author of Faith and Love: Moving Along Through Biblical Truth is an awesome woman of God. Virginia, the oldest girl of 3 children, was born in New York on October 20, 1945. She has been married to Theron Edge since 1979. Virginia is the mother of 3, Grandmother of 7 and Great-grandchildren of 3 she is in the practice of giving sound, motherly well-seasoned advice to her children, Grandchildren, and Great-grandchildren. They have a Yorkie Terrier Maxis Edge 14 years old passed away December 29,2021. She has always had a great love for her family and has poured all that she has into her children and family (and Maxis is no exception).

She has the heart to give, that big heart led her to a career in Nursing. Virginia was a nurse for many years, although she retired over 23 years ago and hasn't slowed down since. Virginia assists with the care of her sister who now is ill.

Virginia is selfless and willing to help those in need. It is in every fiber of her being to do what is right . . . just because that is what God would have her to do. So the principles in Faith & Love are both near and dear to her as well as the way she lives.

She hopes that you will enjoy this book and follow her into future endeavors as she shares the impartation that God has instilled into her life.